Seven Winters in Paris

BY THOMAS McCARTHY

The First Convention
1978

The Sorrow Garden
1981

The Non-Aligned Storyteller
1984

THOMAS McCARTHY

Seven Winters in Paris

Anvil Press Poetry

Published in 1989
by Anvil Press Poetry Ltd
69 King George Street London SE10 8PX

This book is published
with financial assistance from
The Arts Council of Great Britain

Designed and composed by Anvil
Photoset in Baskerville by Wordstream
Printed and bound in England
by The Arc & Throstle Press, Todmorden, Lancs

British Library Cataloguing in Publication Data

McCarthy, Thomas, 1954–
Seven winters in Paris.
I. Title
821'.914

ISBN 0 85646 224 1

FOR THE THREE WISE WILLIAMS:

BILL ROTH

BILL VINCENT

AND IN MEMORY OF BILL SHANNON

ACKNOWLEDGEMENTS

Acknowledgements are due to the following publications in which some of the poems first appeared: *Ambit*, *Belfast Review*, *Field* (Ohio), *Exile* (Toronto), *Poetry Australia*, *Verse*, *Oxford Poetry*, *Orbis*, *The Irish Review*, *The Irish Times*, *The Inherited Boundaries* (edited by Sebastian Barry, The Dolmen Press).

The poem 'The Emigration Trains' is based on the essay 'Oiche na hImirce' by Donal Foley, published in *Scriobh 3*, 1978.

One of the 'wise Williams' to whom this book is dedicated died in late 1988. He was William Shannon, writer, ambassador and historian.

The author gratefully acknowledges the assistance of the American-Irish Foundation, having received their Annual Literary Award in 1984.

CONTENTS

A BOWL OF PEAS

for Catherine

A bowl of freshly depodded peas
is overturned and peas go peppering across the floor,
rat-a-tat, rat-a-tat. The dog follows,
sniffing, and flexing his pliable left ear.

One pea escapes from the impressionist sunlight.
A basket on the window is filled with
freshly picked courgettes and tomatoes,
their colour making a polyptych of stained glass.

There is a smell of woodsmoke. It is autumn
again at Glenshelane, in 1975 or '76.
Our shirts are stained with sweat, our hands grown numb
from the breaking of bonfire wood, the antics

of our old Allen scythe. It is lovely to be
growing into manhood here, to be
like a potter's large vase awaiting fulfilment.
Clay is full of love. There is a blob of light

from the future, like a cuckoo-spit on wild grass.
My whole life was preparing itself for you then.
Your parallel life was like a camera made to pass
over me, tracking roundly, taking it all in.

SEVEN WINTERS IN PARIS

'But the girl I was in love with was in
Paris then, and I did not take the first
train, or the second or the third.'

– HEMINGWAY: A MOVEABLE FEAST

I

Vuillard's hospitable and gifted portraits:
their eyes, passportless,
wandering from Conté to Conté.

II

There was no Thomas MacGreevy waiting
with a stroke of orange in his morning-dress,
but undiplomatic Paris:
fireflies on the rosewood spinet.

III

The bicycles go by in trees and trees
through the dusk of the Invalides.
Raising love-dust, bicycles become leaves –
Marguerite Yourcenar is dead.

IV

Two referenda lost, we took the inner seats
and flew to Paris through wind and sleet.

V

Should we go now, to spread the gospel
of poems, ten Métro tickets surviving
in your purse. For Garret Parnell is dead.

VI

To embrace you, like the Orly security-man:
ah! Irlandais! Your body
is the accent I uncover and uncover.

VII

I am in the Métro beside you thinking
of you faraway in the Métro –
for you have slipped away into a paperback.

VIII

You standing in front of the grey fresco
of Picasso's workshop –
wearing the talisman of a barely pink
scarf, red rag to a bull.

IX

Post-war Elizabeth had just escaped her *Seven Winters*
to fall in love again in Paris.
O Charles Ritchie! Theirs was the high love of mandarins;
the Peace Conference a mere split infinitive.

x

Seven winters in love in Montmartre,
continental snow in the attic glass –
it would be cold cold cold, but dry
enough to keep the Dail out of our hearts.

xi

Even Beckett left behind the malaise
of ourselves by switching tongues.
Love, we withdraw from the mess of the Dail
by flying Aer Lingus to Charles de Gaulle.

xii

The overflowing eyes of Notre-Dame-de-Lorette:
night has been milking the apartments,
loins are feeding in the ninth arrondissement.

xiii

Your soul, when I touch it precisely,
lights up
like the sudden tint of auburn hair.

XIV

I'll be a Sartre to your Simone,
a damaged I, perplexed libido.
But let this be plain:
Paris is a Camus-type, *the wan bliss on the rim.*

XV

Haussmann's boulevards before our eyes,
crown jewels of the radiant Republic.

XVI

Holistically speaking, to love you
is no more difficult than this:
daylight and skylines
in your eyes. Eyes that have this
are always endless.

XVII

Though you are always the best place to write in,
better even than Paris with the forbidding rain,
without back-pain or kidney-pain or heart-pain.

XVIII

While you dress above the shutters and cobbles
the morning sun comes to wash the open pages,
pregnant with leaves – as pregnant
as Ezra Pound in Paris.

XIX

You have rushed before me into daylight
leaving a trail of human leaves –
the light in your hair
would make any Conradh lose its *craobh.*

XX

Let me kiss you on the Balard Line;
we need not take the first or second train.

XXI

And Montmartre will be taken down
and used in evidence.
While the Party fell apart
we wasted centimes at the café of *poésie.*

XXII

The Luxembourg Gardens. A school of chairs
sitting empty, awaiting *Herald Tribune* or *Le Monde*.
A busker makes a hundred notes on solitude.

XXIII

Dead for France, dead for Liberation –
a pock-mark, two pock-marks, near
St Germain-des-Prés:
the splintered cheek-bones of Christ.

XXIV

The Latin Quarter. You are my Héloïse;
only time will tell if I lose my marbles.

XXV

The bicycles speed past Picasso's studio:
horses on their way, pedalling, to see
the thoroughbreds of M. Delacroix.

XXVI

I beat a retreat from St.-John Perse;
his first editions beyond our reach –
sycamore leaves litter the shop-front
like tunic fragments at Austerlitz.

XXVII

Here's the ghost of Ezra Pound,
maestro, tulip-eater,
lost in Arthur Waley and never found.

XXVIII

In the Île de la Cité we meet Denis Devlin,
a polite ghost, remember?
'I hear the poets have lost their marbles,
and the Dail has burned Parnell's heart.'

'Yes, sir. And they were supposed to eat it.'

XXIX

The fever of travel is upon our marriage;
the world is all French when we toss and turn.
Our nerves are alive with it –
Perrier shivers in the tooth-glass.

XXX

The overhead drone in the shallow Métro.
All the haunted traffic of the Gare du Nord;
1848, the first tricolour, Stephens
and Stephen D. 'Parysis, *tu sais*, crucycrooks',
sweet, the honeycomb of exile.

THE GATHERING OF WAVES

The waves gather differently off the coast of Crete;
they are less demented by the inland sea,
though kicked by wind from the Turkish coast.
The sea is grey there, Ottoman, moody.
At Agio Roumeli in the deep south
the shore is red-hot, the sea aquamarine,
plankton-less, like a melting mirror.
The waves are more generous, rhythmic, natal,
like a mould made specially for naked breasts.

You are always heading for the ocean,
unhappy until you can eavesdrop on water
and the waves' conversations.
The sea must be an adequate listener
or an expansive, avuncular teller of tales.
Happy with your feet in water,
you are always calling to me at the shore,
telling me what the sea is,
what a lover can't miss, what the ocean tells you.

Not to understand this is to be a mariner
beached, or a convict on an island
watching the waves gather, listening,
waiting for the one chance to be gathered in.
It is four years, Catherine,
four years that disappear in the sea's mirror.
I see you most clearly then by the ocean,
at Agio Roumeli, you calling me, excited,
wanting to share the salt-water's potable memory.

EDOUARD VUILLARD

1868–1940

Your mother at the window knitting, green drapes;
and outside the soft yellow-stone of Paris;
or your mother watering hyacinths, the floral
tablecloth, reluctant light falling upon her face.
Or your mother at the table, writing,
a cup and newspaper, an ormolu mantle-clock,
or your mother preparing dinner at the rue de Calais.
You painted her through the plethora of cushions:
for your subject was your mother,
the miraculous painter of the household;
the miraculous, trapped, underestimated mother.
What luck you had, Edouard Vuillard,
to know so deeply a trapped untroubled mother,
to leave so beautifully the filial evidence.

Few poets, perhaps Boris Pasternak,
were lucky like this –
and it made of him a huge untoppled romantic:
art, art, art, untoppled romantic.
For who can deny life? Who can deny it
when a child stirs in the womb
like a fine brush stirring on the palette,
when a mother knits finely by lamplight.
For you were never orphaned like us, Party-less,
as orphaned as I felt in the Musée d'Orsay;
orphaned as winter trees in La Place Vintimille.
Your mother at the window, knitting, her green drapes:
one can turn love inside out without loss of style.

HELENA

*

You were as psychic as my father
was confused. Nowadays I am haunted
by you and the menagerie of ghosts –
they are wings of loneliness.

*

Life was a mystery to you –
domestic life was a form of magic:
you always watched the ring of a cooker
as if it was the aurora borealis.

*

A gun behind the picture of The Sacred Heart;
the fear of uniforms. Your half-brother
lost a foot in some Monaghan skirmish –
our poor Republic! The poor always cop it.

*

Why should I love this dead town?
You were humiliated unto death.
Fine Gael wouldn't touch us with a ten-foot
pole, or even a number nine iron.

*

In moments of weakness when I believe in God
instead of the anarchist ideologue, Christ,
I recall the frightening of women by priests,
their Marie Corelli faces, their pitiful beads.

*

You are sitting in my father's lap;
it is a cold day in late October –
you rediscovered each other near the end,
but not before you broke our hearts.

*

I watch the minutes passing away:
the minutes are like bark of *olearia*
blowing along the grass after a storm:
each bark a negative of your dead face.

*

There is a fire burning in the bedroom
the night before my First Communion.
You re-enter, again and again,
to absorb the anointed firelight.

*

To be lucky in love is the best thing,
you insisted. Better than all the wealth
in Dungarvan. Which is why
you switched fiancés at seventeen.

*

I must have seen you crying often
after a Friday morning deluge of bills;
but it is your girl's infectious laugh
that reaches here through the years.

*

Leaves blown against the gutter,
bloodied leaves of Virginia creeper;
an untrained growth is void of conversation,
sterile as an unexamined life.

*

The Dail assembles for a new session;
there's a Deputy still in prison.
How quickly you would have lit candles
for Gregory, as you did for Noel Browne.

*

Suffering anointed you for death.
You were adored at seventeen;
at thirty-seven you had the weight of love –
you were Mary without Elizabeth.

*

I visit your grave for the first time,
Helena, mother. The hardened earth
brings countless humiliations to mind –
no mystical blackbirds, no sparrows.

MERCY HOSPITAL

for David Kiely

I Recovery Room

Dear kidney, now you know it all,
all the folly of a fight
for one sober poet's life –
this feverish April dawn
I watch the gifted nurses,
the ones with Nastassia Kinski eyes,
I watch them inspecting sutures,
replacing drip-feeds, dispensing pethidine.
Their bird-like coming and going,
their trans-wall St Martin de Pores quality
has made me realize
how much I need this life.
Any other Paradise
would be a second-rate surprise.

II Fever

A tall house-officer with long black hair
and a Montenotte accent, but lovely still
with the solace of all that knowledge,
takes a thermometer and sighs.
My room is sick with heat, and sick
with the kindness of so many flowers;
their pungent agricultural *adieu.*

III Sacred Heart

I know I've lost weight already,
suspended from the mean
umbilical of an intravenous drip.
But this is the end of the pain-twilight.
My soul has better hearing,
the body is clairvoyant, soaring
with the loss of pain. The picture
of the Sacred Heart on the wall
has watched over me. It hasn't moved:
you can report this to my cousins,
it hasn't moved from its Italianate
open-heart surgery. You move, though,
from hope to window to hope,
reciting your effective opuscules –
Don't worry
this is not a dry run for a funeral.
And smile. You are the healing Magdalen.

IV VENETIAN LIGHT

My eyes blink and moisten, waking
in the Venetian light
of the first oliguric hours.
There are spots of sunlight on the wall,
disintegrating emboli of dawn.
My body has become the template
of renewal, a more pliable friend.
Much better, thank you. The suffering
Christ on the wall is more distressed-
looking than me, thank God.
Diffuse light that has stirred me
from the multiple nerve-block
of surgery is nothing less
than a consecrated bell
struck by the nescient sister in the corridor.
Pethidine is working still. It clears
the corridors for the Sanctus bell.

V The Shipwreck of Days

To be worried about a friend's poems,
to be restored to a need for friendship,
is the greatest blood-count in the world.
My body is easing away from pain,
it has escaped the cut flowers:
Thank you very much.
I have escaped the haunted hospice.
On my bedside table are Seferis's poems,
the shipwreck of his days in pain.
'It is easier,' he wrote,
'to interview a Cabinet Minister
than to book a surgeon's knife.'
His prayers are on my table now,
sun-drenched, even existentialising
Christ's Passion. *Who knows?*
Going down the neon corridors
of anaesthesia there is nothing, nothing
like 'Mathios Paskalis Among the Roses.'

BEES IN THE RAFTERS

Here I struggle to make a stern diary of love,
Moved by the intimate guest in your womb.

There is a flutter at the centre
Of the sexual paradiso. *Have you felt life?*

Like a mouse stirring among the sheaves
Or rogue honey-bees in the rafters.

But it is something wholly good, the psychic gift
And, also, more like a movement in the heart.

Even the trees are attempting an essay on love
With their red quality-ink of October.

There is a gathering in of everything in
Julie's place because of the rampant summer.

Late bees, drunk with the falling temperature,
Carry their late resources to where we are.

It is easier to speak of death than love;
We're better at idolizing politics than sex.

But I wish to frame the autumn of one mother-to-be,
To make autumnal your summer-loving fertility.

There is a movement at the centre of our days,
Just as the long hot summer moved the country.

Cathy, rogue bees in the rafters, October stores,
Embody the new meaning of what was only words.

LISTENING TO KATE INEZ

I

You frightened the life out of us,
Kate Inez. Bored with growth,
you fell asleep in the womb
or took to reading in the dark.

Little boats out of Helvick,
carrying arms or armless,
never moved as quietly through fluid.
Worried by your silenced voice

we sought the voice that was you,
the fetal heart-beat on a monitor.
The gifted radiographer – all heart,
earth-mother – made you whole.

It was our happy coming-of-age.
We took the afternoon off,
champagned that brief encounter
bathed in the light of ultrasound.

II

Boats creaked along the Libyan Sea
in the month you were conceived.
Our caïque fled the lukewarm food
that was served at Agio Roumeli.

Only the stones were hot,
red-hot with the heat of Cretan sun
and the military jets that blazed
overhead, leaving their sinister trails.

The sea was quiet at Loutron
when the boat cut its engines
and came to rest. Your new mother moved
to the light-drenched bow

to photograph the phosphorescent wharf
while you held on to amoebic life.
Soon this would be a dark sea, with dead
baby Stylianopoulou, dead Hana Gadafy.

III

But you survived it all!
I hear your laughter in the next room.
It's your mother's tickling skill
teasing the graduate of her womb.

She's so skilled at this; an artist,
she could tickle Satan and make
him good. The way she tickled
your father with her artistic limbs

to become a conceiver in the sun,
the way she turned to love, a seal
in the love-ocean. All her good
qualities can become an organic

node of tickling. Your laughter, Kate,
is what you've taken from us both.
But the other thing, the Libyan Sea,
is the unique node of your destiny.

A DAUGHTER'S CRY

At four in the morning we are stirred
by her small insistent night-cry,
like the *ping ping* of a digital clock
in the night air. Her mother
runs before me to staunch the wound
(the night is bleeding strong tears,
the moist cradle is calling for love).
Kate Inez, Kate Inez. Her mother's
weary arms are as strong as motherhood
and coiled against the moonlight,
its natural fawn-like trembling.

When she was born the birds sang
a dawn chorus on Old Blackrock Road.
Nothing stirred but blackbirds
that opened their souls like eyelids,
while we called her name, her name,
across the new, victorious daylight.

CLEANING WHITE SHOES

I GOOD NIGHT

Will you leave the light, Tom? Just a while.
You've already discovered what night means
Now that the bars have come down from your cot;
Nothing to protect you but the brittle
Cobwebby veil of sleep. Four a.m. scenes
And repeated stories are all we've got
To send you back to the enveloping peace.
And where does it come from, this new disease
Of darkness, the fear of the night's unseen?
How many deaths have you witnessed on the small screen
Already, murders while nappy-changing,
Shooting between bottles and Sudocrem?
No Care Bears can protect your naked toes,
No Megan watch the sky while you doze.

II The Month of June

I have *The Irish Times* for the morning
you were born. You are already
part of the archive of my love for you;
a poor archivist, though, my memory is not
steady enough to know what happened.
It was a cold March day, even in the papers,
when you arrived. A Max-Min thermometer
is what I put on your wall instead of the font
of holy water: chance favours those who are
prepared in this world. The world, my love,
is news and news material.
I use an old newspaper on your shoes.
Kate Inez, this is your last month
as our only child. Soon we'll have another
reporter at the nappy-front –
I give you, then, perfectly white shoes
made clean with last Tuesday's news,
a father's tragic love (for love is tragic)
and the bitter-sweet gooseberry month of June.

III OLD CRONIES

The radio crackles on a Minister's words.
What was it you said, my daughter?
More toast, butter my toast. You laugh with me without
knowing why. The Minister
is all blather and blather and blather:
he is what you will grow to despise,
hiding behind an Archbishop;
a poacher among myth, and that perfectly.
When you meet that kind of man, that politics,
may you have the strength to vomit
as the radio vomits now with static,
too old a medium to be fooled by him.
You gulp more milk and listen to the news,
my Sunday morning critic, crony, Kate Inez.
What are you thinking now? Do you think
there must be a poetic form of life,
fatherly and daughterly, intelligent
and beautiful, even for Ireland?
You keep your head and refuse to comment –
toast is your first and second preference.

A DIFFICULT BOY

Slowly the world takes shape around us. Night
and its sisters, moth-wings, streetlamps, recede
quietly and come to rest. You have come to rest,
small boy. You are a bundle of clothes that breathe
and sigh without tension. All the fight
is gone from you. You have acquiesced
while I, night-damaged at thirty-four,
glance through the window at a morning star
and a ship with navigation lights ablaze
slipping downriver on its Conradian journey.
The ocean is elsewhere – out of sight always
like the evasive night of perfect sleep.

A clear day has emerged from the sweaty vapour
of tears, your face composed like a shoreline,
moist and cool as an English water-colour.
Your sleeping mouth whispers '*you're mine, mine* –
dear father, you will walk forever my blazing beam;
you will never jump my ship like Tuan Jim.'

A JULY AFTERNOON ON JAMESON'S FARM

The scents of summer at Tourin,
dappled light on fruit trees.
The farm manager is full of praise
when we strip the bushes clean.
His dog is barking near the jeep
parked at the weighing-shed,
its long tongue a brilliant red
like the skin of July berries.
We are the small *bearachs* in
this life who come to earn their keep
with little hands and plastic cups,
who chafe their white Catholic skins
and mutter insults at each bush
that unleashes a clump of nettles.
One midday we'd already settled
into work when a Southern cloudburst
finished us. For nearly two hours
we sat and played. Our pants were wet
from the leaves deflecting sleet.
Adults went off to the woodstore
for comfort, some lithe teenage girls
coaxed shelter from the tractor lads.
Others went back to Cappoquin
expecting more south-western squalls.

Each July we'd wait for rain to clear,
half-dazed in the moist atmosphere,
until the daughter of the house
raced out with the manager's labrador
to stir workers back to the farm.

Her thick hair was blonde as the sun,
her voice like some homeopathic film
to ease our hail and nettle scars.
Once I was so amazed by her good looks
that I fell headlong into a fruit-box,
covering my face with brilliant juice;
my embarrassment as strong as hate –
her eyes Elizabethan blue, amused.

SUMMER RAIN IN BALLYFERRITER

More flashy July knapsacks gather at Ballyferriter,
church and supermarket still open
to collect whatever pollen of summer business
is still unsettled. Sybil Point
rises and falls among the sisterly hills of mist;
night bobbing like a fishing float,
our minds bobbing, bookless, without ballast.
Our child stirs in her cot. She moves constantly
in her *naomhóg* of sleep while the wind
finds a crevice for its fingers. Windows rattle
and sigh with the strength of young seals.

Dusk falls with the stealth of illegal immigrants:
hundreds of Kerrymen, land-seals of Ballyferriter.
Two have already come home from Boston,
air-coffined home as luck would have it.
Luck like the language is overrun.

Incessant rain still, the thunderous colander
of the sea, a deepening of the *droth-shaol*;
this, and the waffling jurisdiction of the Dail.
Words and their sister, the sea wind,
batter the late nocturnal bog-iris.
Knapsacks flash in the rain, youths disappear in oils.

PERSEPHONE, 1978

The late March mist is an angry Cerberus,
sniffing debris, sniffing the helpless
with its moist noses. The dead are bunched together:
a woman decapitated by a flying wheel-rim,
her daughter screaming 'Help me! Help Mama!'
I crawl through a shattered windscreen
to taste diesel fumes, pungent scattered grain
from the overturned distillery truck.
Arc-lights go on everywhere although
it's still daylight. My eyes hurt. My arms.
My neck is wet, a bloody mist thickening,
a soft March day. There's blood and rain
on the tarmac. Bodies lie stone-quiet
after the catapult of speed.
Even the injured snore deeply. Some will never
come back, never grow warm again.
My mind fills with the constant mutilated dead,
the Ulster dead, the perennial traffic-accident
of Ireland. Here are funerals being made.
A priest walks among the wounded,
Christian stretcher-bearer, helper
and scavenger. My mind fills with hatred.
I race before him to the comatose,
shouting 'You'll be fine! Just keep warm!'
and cover a mother with my duffle-coat.
It is my will against his,
I want to shroud the woman's soul with love,
hesitant, imperfect, but this side of Paradise.
Everywhere is the sound of wailing pain.
A surgeon hurries past, sweating,
his tattered gown is purple with blood,

his face a dark blue narcissus.
I have only words to offer, nothing
like pethidine or the oils of Extreme Unction.
Beside me the woman dies, peppered with barley –
plucked from the insane world like Persephone.

THE EMIGRATION TRAINS, 1943

A pound-note was the best kind of passport
In those days, so I held my pound tight
After my mother turned away. Idlers
Waved farewell from Ferrybank corners.
There was nothing heroic about my going,
Nothing like a political destiny –
I'd just wasted a summer standing round
Until a job came up on the Underground.

I felt destitute, like a vagrant, until
At Waterford station I realized
My good luck: I owned a suitcase of card
While others carried mere bundles of cloth.
At Kilkenny every carriage was filled
To the door. One mother's last grip held fast
Despite the moving train, the rising glass.
For some it was the last touch of a child.

There was nothing pathetic about this:
Look at the Jews, their brave, brave faces –
At least we had our own State to leave from.
Now the emigrant ship was like a big town;
That night it was Clonmel or Cappoquin
With bars open and arguments outdoors,
Politics racing through bleak corridors.

We are heading for England and the world
At war. Neutrality we couldn't afford.
I thought I would spend two years away
But in the end the two became twenty.

Within hours we'd reach the junction at Crewe
And sample powdered eggs from the menu
As well as heavy bombs falling nearby;
All that fatal traffic of an alien sky.

I was so raw and Irish at the time
They said that shamrocks grew out of my ears.
I wasn't alone with my homesick mind:
When we sailed into Holyhead our tears
Made one bitter tide. One labourer's voice
Rose out of the ship like a skylark's,
Singing *Kevin Barry, Kevin Barry*.
His song became our night-cry at the dock.

GLOUCESTER ROAD STATION

I wish you were here in this frantic place
Where women are paved with gold ear-rings
And men are paved with little burdens
Like Harrods bags and Bond Street packages.
This is the bazaar of all our desires,
The foreign city of London. I wish you were here,
I wish we had a credit card.
The man selling ham rolls knows me by now
Because I've been here three days. 'A brown roll'
He says while he opens the cooler-press.
Wide-eyed as Jonah, I walk away. Trains
Glide and clang to a halt, then move away
Quickly in a perfect toy-town arc,
Leaving a trail of blue metallic sparks.

There is a carnival atmosphere. Trains
Pull at my heart like seaside bumpers.
Carnivals were the first erotic islands
In our riverside Peyton Place:
Which is why so many, roused by need, still go.
At Gloucester Road there's human company,
Enough to placate the plovers' Munchian cry
And all our Catholic distress.
So lovely to escape the festering bog
And the cowering Party hack!
Cathy, how much more lovely it would be
If you were in this Underground with me.

You would see the little Indian girl,
Black-eyed, with the red gift of the *Tilak*
On her forehead, and a German woman
Reading a book on the Moselle wine-trade.

You would hear the liquid sitar music
Flowing from the cornucopia of a stall
And, somewhere in the bosom of it all,
The Pyrenean drone of a piccolo:
Which just reminds me of a city that
We shared; the Paris of our honeymoon
With its expensive Invalides ham rolls.
But now I hear a sucking sound. I turn
And nearly kiss two kissing women.
Their passionate lunch-time hair is twisted
In one tight, oblivious lovers' knot.

My feelings for you are all assembled
In their total embrace. The creaking lift
For the District Line clicks shut:
The lovers are pushed apart. Cages shift
And swing. Commuters are settling in.
Cathy, distance makes us very close;
Distance restores the essential spirit,
Which is more than spirit – more feral,
More ferrous, like the movement of trains.
I search the burnt ochre of crowds. You'll
Know what I mean. Lonely, I'm a dishevelled Mick
Caught in a rush-hour cage at Gloucester Road.

BUTTEVANT STATION, 1949

'Tagann fairsinge dochreidte sa tsaol nuair
a imíonn an eagla. Mar níl de dheacracht ar
an saol ach eagla na deachrachta . . . '
– SEÁN Ó RÍORDÁIN

You. You had a good twenty months at home –
such liberation in a time like this!
atomized cities, food-coupons, the McAlpine
trek that is the destiny of Irishmen like us.
Our families were spared that telegram: *Mère décédée.*
Enterrement demain. Sentiments distingués.
We meet again at Buttevant Station –
ah, poet, we've survived the existentialist
intersections, praying daily to the Blessed Virgin.
She has spared us from an entire World War.
Fear nothing, then, but fear and fear and fear.

THE STANDING TRAINS

'. . . and I thought how wonderful to miss one's connections; soon I shall miss them all the time.'

— LOUIS MACNEICE: THE STRINGS ARE FALSE

From the windows of a standing train
you can judge the artwork of our poor Republic.
The prominent ruins that make Limerick Junction
seem like Dresden in 1945
and the beaten-up coaches at Mallow Station,
the rusted side-tracks at Charleville,
have taken years of independent thought.
It takes decades to destroy a system
of stations. On the other hand, a few
well-placed hand-signals can destroy a whole
mode of life, a network of happiness.
This is our own Republic! O Memory,
O Patria, the shame of silenced junctions.
Time knew we'd rip the rails apart, we'd sell
emigrant tickets even while stripping
the ticket-office bare. The standing trains
of the future were backed against a wall.

Two hens peck seed from the bright platform,
hens roost in the signal-box.
Bilingual signs that caused a debate in the Senate
have been unbolted and used as gates:
it's late summer now in this dead station.
When I was twelve they unbolted the rails.
Now there's only the ghost of my father,
standing by the parcel-shed with his ghostly
suitcase. When he sees me walking towards him
he becomes upset. *Don't stop here!* he cries.
Keep going, keep going! This place is dead.

SAN CLEMENTE STATION, 1978

for Bill Roth

The train steams south towards summer
on this mediocre January day,
dull and soft like a Waterford holiday.
Early mist and thin newspapers
make a simple breakfast fare:
news-stands are light with the post-coital
triste of Christmas in the Carter era.
There is a ceiling on public pay
and local fires in Santa Ana,
though mist may spread to save the day.

We have been travelling this Amtrak line,
a beautiful Hispanic girl and I
and two navel cadets from Oregon.
We've slipped through the suburbs of LA,
the back-lots of a million homes,
to exchange used papers, sections
of the *Los Angeles Times*; and complain
about the price of records, rail-tickets,
real estate in the Santa Ana hills.
We lose the suburbs as abruptly
as the mist that clears. The sea, Oceanside,
palm trees, then orange groves appear
like colour slides flung at the train.
At San Clemente Station the waves
murmur across the embankment: water
absorbs a picture of itself pulling in.

Well, I'm home. Our girl companion
gathers her January shopping bags
and turns to go. A bronze surfer

catches her eye through the window
and they smile. I think
of their renewed Pacific sex life.
'You must be happy to be home.'
No. No
I hate coming back to San Clemente,
my mother's on her own, depressed.
While oceanic sunlight floods the train
I think of my father's sudden death.
It's eighteen months now, he died in June.
This is the farthest I've ever been from home.

CATALOGUING TWELVE FENIAN NOVELS

335.04

Dampness has eaten away at *The Dunferry Risin.*
Ninety years have waterlogged the author's name:
Moran is missing, only *J. J.* survives
in the grey fog of the spine –
the author as his mother knew him
or as the IRB might have known him
in the familial secretive world.
It was praised by an MP in *The Evening Sun*,
generous in Victorian London's neutrality.
This is the best picture ever of the IRB.

398.21

Lennox, should we move you from fiction to 398?
For years you haven't moved from the fiction shelf;
your *A Young Man from the South* is brown with rot,
should we throw it out? The folklore
that coloured your pen was overwhelming
and overwhelmed so many with love –
love of country is such a blessed thing,
Fay's Abbey Theatre, Yeats' *Kathleen Ni Houlihan.*
We've moved from Willie to Enoch Powell,
from the soft porn of Lennox consumed
to the steel horn, hard as Wolverhampton nails.
Lennox, welcome to the sceptical librarian
who hauls you out of time, fiction and pain.

941.591

Rain seeps through the hoarding on the broken window;
Corkery rain, insistent, dramatic.
Youths are playing darts against the library
door, challenging me to respond:
public servant, hated. Bull's eye!
Tina, these two are gone mouldy, will I
throw them out? A note from Sheila
attached to *The Whiteboys* by Mrs S. C. Hall
and D. M. Lenihan's *The Red Spy* –
the red spy a Dublin Castle agent
forever on the threshold of quiet, of death.

364.

This is what fiction can do to a country:
a battle-cruiser in the Gulf, destroyers off Blackpool
for the Conservative conference. Who will
unwind the paranoia? The poets? The courts,
God help us. There is the question of the Birmingham Six,
Diplock Courts, the literally bloody mess
left by a murdered machine, botched revolution.
Too many brushes with the wrong tribunal –
I commit Canon Sheehan
to the library trash-can,
seven pages missing from his *Glenanaar*
as pages have fallen away from the statute books
to expose the raw powers of the State.
Too late to save *Glenanaar*, its conspirators,
the late Canon's quality of remembrance.
This is what terror can do to a novelist.

920.BAR

George Bartram, this can't be your life-story;
Fisher Unwin's *White-Headed Boy*
that has languished in the biography section
for twenty years, another Irish tale
to satiate the post-Pre-Raphaelites.
Bertram, who are your children's children?
Did you know the Sinn Fein candidate,
Louis Walsh – the South Derry hopeful?
– Louis has drawn a pen-portrait of '48,
The Next Time, with O'Connell, Duffy, Davis.
The whole of our lives, a hundred years
of biography masquerading as novels
and novelists moonlighting as MPs.
Ours was an abrupt and botched revolution;
coitus interruptus, impermanent as binding-wax.

327.415

Power after absolution, chimeric prestige,
prison is the perfect background for an MP.
When We Were Boys is what William O Brien
made of two years inside.
Longmans in the '90s, then Maunsel in '18
bought his Glengarrif story.

O distant country!
O broken dreams!
For liberation is a valley of disappointment –
after power, the mere excitement of museums.

630.

The past is so rural and intimate, if we forget
the rotted corpse in ditch-water, hooded
and whole streets disembowelled like spineless books.
The past has charm like cut glass or wickerwork:
beware of novelists throwing or weaving that –
Alexander MacArthur's *Irish Rebels* or Lysaght's
Her Majesty's Rebels, their stress of contradictions
like the stress at the apex of heavy thatch.
Their spines have fallen apart, and their stories
withered. Rotted cords, decaying sallie-rods.
They wished to keep two things going at once,
the aesthetic being and the ethnic predicament.
Mr Lysaght, your book is committed to the *worn-out* bin
– like our view of history, from Davis to 1891.

823.BER

The hard cover of this novel comes away in my hand,
the desecrations of time,
like the desecration of farms and great houses
for the common good.
Mr Butler of *The Bad Times* was hauled
into truth, manhandled, as disappointed as Isaac Butt.
For the liberal mind cannot stand violence
as the propertied abhor agrarian unrest –
what is it that we cannot bear to lose?
Binding thread hangs from this damaged book
as corpses hung, feather-like,
from the unpainted gibbet of the nineteenth century.
Our past was in these words, *The Bad Times*
as quiet now as the hanging man without land.

821.LAW

Sweet daughter of our Lord Cloncurry, Emily
Lawless, you wrote *Hurrish* in a hurry
and it flourished for you, for years.
What right did you have to make such fiction
out of death? Was your heart with the Land League?
I'd say not:
no more than the true heart of Longfellow
was in the breast of the Indian princess.
Now the world is bleak, by café or lake.
I can only think your mutilated book
is a song like Hiawatha's,
so dark we must eat our fear together.

THE DYING SYNAGOGUE AT SOUTH TERRACE

Chocolate-coloured paint and the July sun
like a blow-torch peeling off
the last efforts of love:
more than time has abandoned this,
God's abandonment, God's synagogue,
that rose out of the ocean
one hundred years from here.
The peeling paint is an immigrant's
guide to America – lost on the shore
at Cobh, to be torn and scored
by a city of *luftmenshen*,
Catholics equally poor, equally driven.

To have been through everything,
to have suffered everything and left
a peeling door. *Yahweh* is everywhere,
wherever abandonment is needed –
a crow rising after a massacre,
wearing the grey uniform
of a bird of carrion, a badger
waiting for the bones of life
to crack before letting go:
wishing the tenth cantor to die,
the synagogue to become a damp wall,
the wailing mouths to fester.
Too small. To be a small people
aligned to nothing is to suffer blame
like a thief in the night. Some activist
throws a bomb for the suffering PLO:

the sky opens and rains a hail
like snowdrops. Flowers for memory,
petrol for the faraway.
To define one's land is to be a cuckoo
pushing others, bird-like, into a pit,
until at the end every national gesture
becomes painful, soiling the synagogue
door, like the charcoal corpses
at Mauthausen Station, 1944.

We who did nothing for you, who
remained aloof with the Catholic world
and would have cried *Jew!* like the others –
David forgive us –
we who didn't believe the newsreels,
preferring hatred of England to love of you,
we might shut our hypocrite mouths,
we want a West Bank but not a Stormont.
We have no right over your batons,
having made nothing for you but L. Bloom.

To sit here now in the rancid sunshine
of low tide is to interiorize
all of the unnoticed work of love –
exquisite children fall like jewels
from an exhausted colporteur's bag;
a mid-century daughter practises piano,
an *étude* to cancel terror; a nephew
dreams of the artistic life, another
shall practise law and become, in time,
the Catholic's tall Lord Mayor.
Where these jewels fall beside the peeling door
let us place the six lilies of memory;
the six wounds of David's peeling star.

CIMETIÈRE PÈRE LACHAISE

for John Montague

Nearby, the graves of genius: Wilde, de Nerval, Éluard.
Rusting leaves turn like prejudice playing hide-and-seek.
Before me, the Mauthausen Memorial. Built upon tears.
It is a damned lie to say that they were murdered
for freedom's sake, or for the glory of France –
they died because the heart of religion was rotten,
and the heart of Europe. It's grotesque
to mention glory. Say instead *Himmler* or *auto da fé*,
say Madrid, 1680, eighteen Marranos burned to death
to celebrate the wedding of Carlos and Marie Louise:
and Madame d'Aulnay, 'The courage with which the Jews
went to their deaths aroused general amazement . . . '

Père Lachaise, the tricolour ribbons of the Republic
bind up our Catholic penance of hot-house flowers.

THINKING OF MY FATHER
IN THE MUSÉE PICASSO

It breaks my heart to think of your failures,
for you were not a bad man, just hopeless.
The lost Party, those lethal social forces
that broke your will broke others less poor.
Talent is a muscle that needs constant exercise
and Ireland was your disagreeable milieu –
all the end-of-term banter of the Dail
couldn't hide that truth. But look at Picasso:
he was a bullish, besieged Stalinist,
yet he worked and worked and worked.
Every butterfly of an idea he embraced became art;
and every false move he made used material
more permanent and beautiful than the Dail.

PICASSO'S 'COMPOSITION AU PAPILLON'

When I contemplate your magic gifts tonight,
alone, the back-boiler creaking, the frosty moonlight,
I am reminded that you were Leonardo
reincarnate, the Cuchulain of canvas.
Paint never buckled under such pressure –
Guernica, vulgar goats, the portraits of Olga;
even something as brittle as 'Composition au Papillon'
has the finished look to make gods finite.

In Paris, at fifty-one, you could play God
with cloth, string, a thumb-tack, oil. Truth is
we are all born to an artless, provincial stench.
If we are lucky, Picasso, we die French.

HUGH MACDIARMID

Here on the Celtic fringe ice is very thin;
if you speak a word of English I'll fall in,
into the *muckle toon* of florid talk,
the quagmire of manners, the velvet catwalk
of bourgeois courtesy. Let us kiss each other
on the arse for luck, and not stir
again until I've praised as best I can
your own gift, and your genius, Scotland.
How you suffered at the hands of others,
dear Chris! The air was very thin
between cabins, the kirk too full of nerves
to challenge those who came to burn and sin.
Dr Grieve, remember the good luck
of having a postman for a father
and a post-office full of Victorian books
to cheer you while you waited there.
Scotland's past was a parcel of ill-luck,
with you, its covering letter, gone astray.
History can't close on the Sabbath Day,
nor poetry. They festered in the volumes
that you took away. Poor man's child, say
'I'm sorry. I know too much for my age.
My bourgeois teachers are in a rage.'

The sentimental masters would have you praise
our unique Celticness, the infinite
boredom of the picturesque, braes
at break of day. I can hear you say
'What about the slums, the insomniac
nature of poverty and disease?'

You had a continent elsewhere
to write about: Stalin's land
that you and they could barely understand.

As Benedict of Clusa used to say
to the troublesome Bishops of Aquitaine
'I have two houses full of books,
I meditate upon them every day.'

How much of Scotland fell apart
when you broke down, how many mere tits' eggs
that would have pleased the pious kirk?
More natural achievements took their place:
a winter mezereum, differential calculus,
that dragged you into a wider arc
to stare amazed at the mere *material.*
There, on the material fringe, the ice
was very thin. You swallowed more
than Scotland whole when you jumped in.

IN ARMENIA, 1988

My little son cries out in the night.
Teething or chicken-pox, what does it matter
when age itself is the only cure
and adulthood the only true inoculation.
My child without speech
is not a good night companion,
his opinions still out of reach,
locked in the brilliant gourd
of his red hair, chicken-poxed hairline.
Yet he is everything that is hopeful in me,
the way one hopes for a second beginning
to make things perfect: a promising
New Year, an unscratched lottery ticket.

How much more vulnerable is the unknown child
in Armenia? I think of the unknown son
crying in the rubble (the street photographers missed),
his nose blocked with the ash of the earth,
with terror broken loose from unstitched rock
and him fatherless, beyond laughter,
at the burning hairline of the earth.

NOTES

These notes are not meant to be definitive, but merely indicators for non-Irish readers.

SEVEN WINTERS IN PARIS

Conradh: League.
craobh: branch.

A JULY AFTERNOON ON JAMESON'S FARM

bearachs: migrant workers brought into Waterford from West Cork by Protestant colonists in the seventeenth century.

SUMMER RAIN IN BALLYFERRITER

naomhóg: Kerry Gaelic term for a boat made of wood and skin.

droth-shaol: an expression used by old country people to describe the hard life of the past.

BUTTEVANT STATION, 1949

Epigraph: 'An incredible spaciousness comes into life when fear departs. For there is no difficulty in life like the fear of difficulty.'